ALSO BY J. D. McCLATCHY

POETRY

Ten Commandments   1998
The Rest of the Way   1990
Stars Principal   1986
Scenes from Another Life   1981

ESSAYS

Twenty Questions   1998
White Paper   1989

AS EDITOR

Horace: The Odes   2002
Bright Pages: Yale Writers 1701–2001   2001
Longfellow: Poems and Other Writings   2000
The Vintage Book of Contemporary World Poetry   1996
Woman in White: Poems by Emily Dickinson   1991
The Vintage Book of Contemporary American Poetry   1990
Poets on Painters   1988
Recitative: Prose by James Merrill   1986
Anne Sexton: The Poet and Her Critics   1978

(with Stephen Yenser)
James Merrill: Collected Novels and Plays   2002
James Merrill: Collected Poems   2001

AS TRANSLATOR

Carmen   2001
The Magic Flute   2000

HAZ

MAT

haz POEMS

J. D. McCLATCHY

ALFRED A. KNOPF   NEW YORK   2004

mat

THIS IS A BORZOI BOOK
PUBLISHED BY ALFRED A. KNOPF

www.randomhouse.com/knopf/poetry

Owing to limitations of space, all acknowledgments for
permission to print previously published material may
be found at the end of the book.

Knopf, Borzoi Books, and the colophon are registered
trademarks of Random House, Inc.

Library of Congress Cataloging-in-Publication Data

McClatchy, J. D., 1945–
    Hazmat / by J. D. McClatchy.
      p. cm.
    ISBN 0-375-70991-6 (pbk.)
      1. Body, Human—Poetry.   I. Title.
    PS3563.A26123 H39 2002
    813'.54—dc21   2002020529

Manufactured in the United States of America
Published, October 30, 2002
First Paperback Edition, April 9, 2004

for Chip Kidd

CONTENTS

I.

II.

I.

FADO

Suppose my heart had broken
Out of its cage of bone,
Its heaving grille of rumors—
    My metronome,

My honeycomb and crypt
Of jealousies long since
Preyed on, played out,
    My spoiled prince.

Suppose then I could hold it
Out towards you, could feel
Its growling hound of blood
    Brought to heel,

Its scarred skin grown taut
With anticipating your touch,
The tentative caress
    Or sudden clutch.

Suppose you could watch it burn,
A jagged crown of flames
Above the empty rooms
    Where counterclaims

Of air and anger feed
The fire's quickening flush
And into whose remorse
    Excuses rush.

Would you then stretch your hand
To take my scalding gift?
And would you kiss the blackened
    Hypocrite?

It's yours, it's yours—this gift,
This grievance embedded in each,
Where time will never matter
    And words can't reach.

G L A N U M

_____

at the ruins of a provincial Roman town

So this is the city of love.
I lean on a rail above
Its ruined streets and square
Still wondering how to care
For a studiously unbuilt site
Now walled and roofed with light.
A glider's wing overhead
Eclipses the Nike treads
On a path once freshly swept
Where trader and merchant kept
A guarded company.
As far as the eye can see
The pampered gods had blessed
The temples, the gates, the harvest,
The baths and sacred spring,
Sistrum, beacon, bowstring.
Each man remembered his visit
To the capital's exquisite
Libraries or whores.
The women gossiped more
About the one-legged crow
Found in a portico
Of the forum, an omen
That sluggish priests again
Insisted required prayer.

A son's corpse elsewhere
Was wrapped in a linen shroud.
A distant thundercloud
Mimicked a slumping pine
That tendrils of grape entwined.
Someone kicked a dog.
The orator's catalogue
Prompted worried nods
Over issues soon forgot.
A cock turned on a spit.
A slave felt homesick.
The underclass of scribes
Was saved from envy by pride.
The always invisible legion
Fought what it would become.

. . .

We call it ordinary
Life—banal, wary,
Able to withdraw
From chaos or the law,
Intent on the body's tides
And the mysteries disguised
At the bedside or the hearth,
Where all things come apart.
There must have been a point—
While stone to stone was joined,
All expectation and sweat,
The cautious haste of the outset—
When the city being built,
In its chalky thrust and tilt,
Resembled just for a day

What's now a labeled display,
These relics of the past,
A history recast
As remarkable rubble,
Broken column, muddled
Inscription back when
Only half up, half done.
Now only the ruins are left,
A wall some bricks suggest,
A doorway into nothing,
Last year's scaffolding.
By design the eye is drawn
To something undergone.
A single carving remains
The plunder never claimed,
And no memories of guilt
Can wear upon or thrill
This scarred relief of a man
And woman whom love will strand,
Their faces worn away,
Their heartache underplayed,
Just turning as if to find
Something to put behind
Them, an emptiness
Of uncarved rock, an excess
Of sharp corrosive doubt.

. . .

Now everything's left out
To rain and wind and star,
Nature's repertoire
Of indifference or gloom.

This French blue afternoon,
For instance, how easily
The light falls on debris,
How calmly the valley awaits
Whatever tonight frustrates,
How quickly the small creatures
Scurry from the sunlight's slur,
How closely it all comes to seem
Like details on the table between
Us at dinner yesterday,
Our slab of sandstone laid
With emblems for a meal.
Knife and fork. A deal.
Thistle-prick. Hollow bone.
The olive's flesh and stone.

LARGESSE

It begins with an apple offered, a shy smile,
  A desire as yet half-satisfied.
The shame comes later, when finally betrayed
  By a joy the giver all the while
Has taken in fears that vanity provides.
    What might have gone, been lost, has stayed.

But feelings change, our needs are met or not,
  The chip-stacked gaming table's rigged.
What's given has a history of its own.
  A silent partner was bribed or shot.
A harried client misplaced her thingamajig.
    That rivière was rhinestones.

You don't know where it's been, my mother said,
  And slapped the sidewalk nickel out
Of my mouth. How else acquire a taste for all
  The world would give, its fairy bread
And goblin fruit, its initial germ of doubt
    No dire warnings could forestall?

From brimming nipple to crematory flame,
  We give ourselves to what will take
The breath away. The queen throws unstrung pearls
  From a balcony, or Jove campaigns
In showers of gold, and who can stay awake?
    But the prince's hand, the shortstop's girl

With her legs apart, or half the saint's own cloak . . .
        The beggar in each of us is roused.
The problem then is how to give away
        The gift. A charity provoked
By guilt is straw in the fire compassion avows.
        I am meant to offer with no display

The what-I-am instead of the what-I-have,
        All of it, the manic and mean,
And then to stand aside the better to mull
        On blowsy Fortune nodding off
Behind the wheel of her gilded, greased machine,
        and Mary Magdalene holding her skull.

TANKAS

_____

Who is now as young
As a love letter's first fold?
Still, this gift . . . wrapped in a cloud,

The curvature of his comb
A mark of favor—but whose?

· · ·

The geisha's stinger
Wavers in the crucifix
On her pashmina.

Further reflection yields—look!—
Her half-lit Lark and magnate.

· · ·

The courtiers say
The household lacks a certain
Reticence taken

To extremes, as in those days
When the moon was never praised.

· · ·

The Starbucks counter.
A pierced, swishy, tie-dyed head,
His finger stirring

A latte, jokes with the monk
About saffron withdrawal.

· · ·

Today's rehearsal
Of yesterday has gone well
Enough to postpone

Tomorrow's first performance.
I told them I hate my lines.

· · ·

Next, my waitress at
The No-Panties Coffee Shop
Embarrasses me.

Quickly I look away, down
To the mirror-floor's rebuke.

· · ·

The prince, suddenly
Grown up, visits the palace.
His old wet-nurse weeps.

How he hides his foolishness
With attendants and a scowl.

     • • •

The Atomic Bomb
At the pachinko arcade,
With deadly pinball

Accuracy, first lights up,
Then pays off in dummy coins.

     • • •

She blackens her teeth,
Powders her face, and pinches
The hem of her silks.

Tonight she will take her place.
They are casting out demons.

     • • •

At the Deep-See Baths
I swim against schools headed
From steam to salt rub

To scalding herbal falls, back
Towards the locker room's cool shoals.

. . .

My brush flickers through
The water in my inkstone.
Even the sutra

Stumbles, its only lantern
The Buddha's fading gold foil.

.

J I H A D

A contrail's white scimitar unsheathes
Above the tufts of anti-aircraft fire.
Before the mullah's drill on righteousness,
Practice rocks are hurled at chicken-wire

Dummies of tanks with silhouetted infidels
Defending the nothing both sides fight over
In God's name, a last idolatry
Of boundaries. The sirens sound: take cover.

He has forced the night and day, the sun and moon,
Into your service. By His leave, the stars
Will shine to light the path that He has set

You to walk upon. His mercy will let
You slay who would blaspheme or from afar
Defile His lands. Glory is yours, oh soon.

Of the heart. Of the tongue. Of the sword. The holy war
Is waged against the self at first, to raze
The ziggurat of sin we climb upon
To view ourselves, and next against that glaze

The enemies of faith will use to disguise
Their words. Only then, and at the caliph's nod,

Are believers called to drown in blood the people
Of an earlier book. There is no god but God.

He knows the day of death and sees how men
Will hide. Who breaks His covenant is cursed.
Who slights His revelations will live in fire.

He has cast aside the schemer and the liar
Who mistake their emptiness of heart for a thirst
That, to slake, the streams of justice descend.

Ski-masked on videotape, the skinny martyr
Reads his manifesto. He's stilted, nervous.
An hour later, he's dropped at the market town,
Pays his fare, and climbs aboard the bus.

Strapped to his chest is the death of thirty-four
—Plus his own—"civilians" on their way
To buy or sell what goods they claim are theirs,
Unlike our fates, which are not ours to say.

Under the shade of swords lies paradise.
Whom you love are saved with you, their souls
In His hand. And who would want to return to life

Except to be killed again? Who can thrive
On the poverty of this world, its husks and holes?
His wisdom watches for each sacrifice.

ORCHID

_____

Now that you are gone, you are everywhere.
        Take this orchid, for instance,
its swollen lip, the scrawny stalk's one
        descended testicle
as wrinkled as rhetoric on the bar-scene stump,
        the golden years since
jingling in its purse. How else signal the bee?

In my swan-clip now languish urgent appeals
        from the usual charities
lined up to be ignored. But your flags are up:
        I see the flapping petals,
the whorl of sepals, their grinning come-on.
        Always game, again
I'd head straight for the column's sweet trap.

Ducking under the puckered anther cap
        to glide towards the stiff,
waxy sense of things, where male and female
        hardly matter to one's heady
urge to pull back the glistening lobes
        and penetrate the heart,
I fell for it every time, the sticky bead

laid down on my back as I huddled there
        with whatever—mimicking
enemy or friend, the molecular musk

of each a triggering lure—
wanted the most of me. Can I leave now too?
    I have death's dust-seed
on me. I have it from touching you.

CANCER

1.

And then a long senescent cell—though why,
Who knows?—will suddenly refuse to stay
In line, the bucket brigade of proteins meant
To slow or stimulate the tissue's growth
Will stumble, so the cells proliferate
And tumors form while, deep within,
Suppressor genes, mutated, overlook
The widening fault, the manic drive to choke
On itself that fairy tales allot the gnome
Who vainly hammers the broken sword in his cave,
Where malignant cells are shed into the blood
Or lymph, cascading through the body's streams,
Attaching themselves to places where we breathe
And love and think of what cannot be true.

2.

It is as if, the stench intensified
And strong or weak alike now swept away,
The plague in Athens hurried its descent
By fear, a symptom leaving the stricken loath
To fight for life who had defied the great
Spartan ranks themselves, the sight of skin
Inflamed, the thirst, the dripping anus took

Hold of them until, in tears, they broke.
The dead in piles around them, a hecatomb
To gods who, like those mongrel dogs who crave
A corpse they drag to safety through the mud
To feast upon, had disappeared, their dreams,
According to Thucydides, seethed
With images of forsaken, drowning crews.

3.

She had lost the bet, and in her sunken eyes
The birthday she had over and over prayed
To die before was offered like a present.
(Dressed in a party hat, I sat with both
My parents by the bed.) A toast was made.
Through the pleated, angled straw she took in
A burning mouthful of champagne, and rebuked
Her son-in-law for his expensive joke,
Drawing, hairless, an imaginary comb
Through memories of what pleasure anger gave,
Then smiled, "I'd stop all this if only I could."
Even at ten I sensed that she had seen,
Staring at me, what would be bequeathed.
My mother slowly closed her eyes. We knew.

E L B O W S

_____

If David's foot rests on the giant's head—
        Gingerly, we assume, since the whole earth
            Is now its body—the hand on his hip
        Points casually away from the combat,
The tensed slingshot now an arm akimbo.

            The fingers of sincerity lightly grazing
        the chest, the salesman's handshake, the boxer's fist,
the palms-up appeal—none has the nonchalance
    of the CEO, a plate-glass window behind,
            patron in his own commissioned altarpiece,

the hitched Armani shirt sleeves crossed or jutting,
        the more off the cuff to highlight his holdings.
            Always certain they are covered from behind,
        our standard bearers, Sir Swank or Lady World,
one elbow pouting, to the camera's eye aggressively

        relaxed, rub them with each other's,
    while a free hand holds the war hammer
or electric guitar. The rest of us need to keep ours
    off the table and away from anyone's ribs
        but a friend's. We need ours to rest on

while we think, or seem to be doing so. And of what?
    Of stretching out sideways on rumpled sheets,

head propped up to gaze warily
on that day's beloved at last asleep beside you.
Then you turn, put your arms at your side, and stare up.

PENIS

———————

Years of sneaking sidelong glances towards the one
    At the next urinal's gaping mouth—
Between classes, between buses, between acts,
    In dorm or disco, rest stop or Ritz—
Assemble them now in a sort of line-up:
    Bald, one-eyed, red-faced, shifty suspects,
Each generic, all so individual—
    Hooded, lumpish, ropy, upcurving,
Anchovy or shark, the three-inch alley cat
    Or blood-choked panther whose last droplet,
Back-lit by porcelain, is wagged free to fly
    In a bright sterile arc, its reversed
Meniscus shattered by the soon swirling flush.
    But that slice-of-life in the Men's Room
In retrospect seems an idle pantomime,
    Old desires or anxieties
Projected onto a stranger's handful
    Of gristle, the shadowy dumb show
Our schoolroom puppets once swooped and wiggled through
    Back when any sense of difference
Posed as curiosity's artless cut-outs.
    Only years later was I haunted
By a premonition of something I thought
    I didn't have, or have enough of
—Poor Punch, fingered, limp, flung back into his case.

        • • •

Who knows what early memories are redeemed,
    What primitive rites re-enacted,

By our masculine version of mother-love?
    What daily unconscious tenderness
Is lavished here, such fastidious grooming
    Rituals for the wrinkled baby
Capuchin. Each man's member every morning
    May be gingerly held and juggled
Inside his Jockey shorts or lazily scratched
    Through silk pajamas—in any case,
Fondled, its puckered, sweat-sticky, fetid skin
    Lifted off the scrotal water-bed
And hand-dried as if in a tumbler of air.
    Later, tucked behind the clerk's apron
Or the financier's pinstripes or the rapper's
    Baggy jeans, our meek little Clark Kent
Daydreams at his desk of last night's heroics,
    Hounded by a double life blackmailed
By grainy color shots of summer-cabin
    Or backseat exploits that had won praise
From their pliant, cooing co-conspirators.
    But now, absently readjusted,
As if fresh from cold surf, his ideal is just
    The bud of classic statuary.
The marble is hard, the soulful cub withdrawn.

        • • •

So, the old questions linger on unanswered.
    Why in the fables on Greek kraters
Do those of the ephebes always stick straight out?
    Why is it the last part of a man's
Body to age? Though function may no longer
    Follow form, its chthonic shaft and crown
Retain maturity's rugged majesty.
    What Ovid might once have figured out

As a shepherd who'd struck a king in disguise,
    Or Plato have thought in an aside
The haphazard tail of white in the pot where
    His abstract egg was hard-boiling into halves
Soon in search of some way to resume the shell
    Of an identical privacy,
Scientists today measure as Anyman's
    Lowest common denominator,
A demonic's tutorial in the means
    Of his being manipulated
By unpredictable powers far beyond
    His knowing but not his sad sensing.
Do I wish my own rose at will, and stayed put,
    And was just, say, two inches longer?
Sure. So who doesn't think he's inherited
    An apartment too small for his plans?
Do I cancel the party, or gamely shrug?

        • • •

"But why," Jane asks, "is something silly at best
    And objectively ugly at worst
The focus of so much infatuation?"
    Cults thrive on cloying contradictions.
Shrewd and aloof, women are thought to enjoy
    What it does, the petulant master
They devour, or the wheedling spongy slave
    They finally love to rub the wrong way.
And men? Men! Men are known to appreciate
    What it stands for. History books have this
In common with off-the-rack pulp romances.
    Small men with big ones, big men with small,
Lead lives of quiet compensation, power
    Surging up from or meekly mizzling

Down to the trouser snake in their paradise.
    If love's the religion with the god
That fails, is it because blood goes to his head?
    No, it's that after the night's tom-toms
And fire-dances are over and he's sulking
    In his shrine, sadness beats him hollow.
Asked by nagging reporters once too often
    Why, despite the count of body bags,
We were in Vietnam, LBJ unzipped
    His fly and slapped it on the table.
"Gentlemen, this is why," he barked. "This is why."

F E C E S

　　The evidence,
if it is merely waste, suggests
　　what I had once been shown—
　　　the monitor's

　　worm's-eye view up
the overstrung tunnel my guide—
　　that the body most wants
　　　an empty tomb,

　　a place to fill
with the next day, the nurturing
　　nothingness it turns into
　　　with time. Why not

　　admit the smell
is of sin, the tainted riches
　　circulating daily?
　　　O dull gold coin,

　　privately held
and publicly spent, heaped, hoarded,
　　the emblem of ego,
　　　my steaming yam,

how easily
I profit from the principle:
Corruption empowers.
My street is paved

with it. Or else
"He reeks of money!" they will say,
as if both to savor
and disapprove.

It makes more sense
to brush aside the sticks and stones
aimed at earshot, and put
my dirty glass

to the flocked wall-
paper by my bed and listen
to the groans and gurglings
of my own past.

When Nature called,
my business was behind closed doors.
Approval—my mother's
must count the most—

is the hidden
agenda, accumulating
by my spoils her favor.
The blood of Christ

might do as well,
or water Pilate used to rinse
his jest away, but mine
is thought clearer—

by me, at least.
What I eliminate today
ushers in an absence,
a purity,

and in the end
a corpse, another left-over
to disinfect, bury,
then finally

identify
with a permanent mortal stench,
the odor of my race.
Or so the myth

gets credited.
At nine—young enough to believe
in stories, old enough
to stand in dread

of something owed
to death—I would save mine, layered
in a plastic bucket,
to keep, to store

in an attic
closet stocked with unwanted lamps
and Christmas ornaments.
Tissue-wrapped balls

of red and green,
unopened packets of tinsel,
metallic pinecones, chipped
Old Father Times

and Madonnas—
the clutter now become a shrine
for my little monstrance.
Here I would come

to undertake
the experimental tasting
and languid inhalings
of what I had

been, what had been
through me, in me, nearer my *self*
than *I* could ever be.
But why the need

not just to guard
but secretly to imagine
all this would someday yield
the upper hand?

And why worship
what had been stolen from myself
    rather than take my seat?
      Nothing festered.

      Nothing was lost.
Within a week the mess had dried
    into a brick the size
      of an idea

    carried around
ever since. Capitalism
    thrives on needs satisfied,
      losses thwarted,

    its retentive,
delirious claim to matter.
    Mine was in the closet.
      Discovery

    followed, of course,
and punishment, and worried looks.
    Already she knew what
      I would become.

TATTOOS

1.

CHICAGO, 1969

Three boots from Great Lakes stumble arm-in-arm
        Past the hookers
    And winos on South State
To a tat shack. Pissed on mai tais, what harm
        Could come from the bright slate
Of flashes on the scratcher's corridor
Wall, or the swagger of esprit de corps?

Tom, the freckled Hoosier farmboy, speaks up
        And shyly points
    To a four-inch eagle
High over the Stars and Stripes at sunup.
        A stormy upheaval
Inside—a seething felt first in the groin—
Then shoves its stubby subconscious gunpoint

Into the back of his mind. The eagle's beak
        Grips a banner
    Waiting for someone's name.
Tom mumbles that he'd like the space to read
        FELIX, for his small-framed

Latino bunkmate with the quick temper.
Felix hears his name and starts to stammer—

He's standing there beside Tom—then all three
            Nervously laugh
        Out loud, and the stencil
Is taped to Tom's chest. The needle's low-key
        Buzzing fusses until,
Oozing rills of blood like a polygraph's
Lines, there's a scene that for years won't come off.

Across the room, facedown on his own cot,
            Stripped to the waist,
        Felix wants Jesus Christ
Crucified on his shoulder blade, but not
        The heartbroken, thorn-spliced
Redeemer of punk East Harlem jailbait.
He wants light streaming from the wounds, a face

Staring right back at those who've betrayed him,
            Confident, strong,
        With a dark blue crewcut.
Twelve shading needles work around the rim
        Of a halo, bloodshot
But lustrous, whose pain is meant to prolong
His sudden resolve to fix what's been wrong.

(Six months later, a swab in Vietnam,
            He won't have time
        To notice what's been inked

At night onto the sky's open hand—palms
     Crawling with Cong. He blinks.
Bullets slam into him. He tries to climb
A wooden cross that roses now entwine.)

And last, the bookish, acned college grad
       From Tucson, Steve,
     Who's downed an extra pint
Of cut-price rye and, misquoting Conrad
     On the fate of the mind,
Asks loudly for the whole nine yards, a "sleeve,"
An arm's-length pattern of motives that weave

And eddy around shoals of muscle or bone.
       Back home he'd signed
     On for a Navy hitch
Because he'd never seen what he's since grown
     To need, an *ocean* which . . .
But by now he's passed out, and left its design
To the old man, whose eyes narrow, then shine.

By dawn, he's done. By dawn, the others too
       Have paid and gone.
     Propped on a tabletop,
Steve's grappling with a hangover's thumbscrew.
     The bandages feel hot.
The old man's asleep in a chair. Steve yawns
And makes his way back, shielded by clip-ons.

In a week he'll unwrap himself. His wrist,
      A scalloped reef,
        Could flick an undertow
Up through the tangled swash of glaucous cyst
      And tendon kelp below
A vaccination scallop's anchored seaweed,
The swelling billow his bicep could heave

For twin dolphins to ride towards his shoulder's
      Coppery cliffs
      Until the waves, all flecked
With a glistening spume, climb the collar-
      Bone and break on his neck.
When he raises his arm, the tide's adrift
With his dreams, all his watery what-ifs,

And ebbs back down under the sheet, the past,
      The uniform.
      His skin now seems colder.
The surface of the world, he thinks, is glass,
      And the body's older,
Beckoning life shines up at us transformed
At times, moonlit, colorfast, waterborne.

2.

Figuring out the body starts with the skin,
    Its boundary, its edgy go-between,
The scarred, outspoken witness at its trials,

The monitor of its memories,
Pleasure's flushed archivist and death's pale herald.
    But skin is general-issue, a blank
Identity card until it's been filled in
    Or covered up, in some way disguised
To set us apart from the beasts, whose aspects
    Are given, not chosen, and the gods
Whose repertoire of change—from shower of gold
    To carpenter's son—is limited.
We need above all to distinguish ourselves
    From one another, and ornament
Is particularity, elevating
    By the latest bit of finery,
Pain, wardrobe, extravagance, or privation
    Each above the common human herd.
The panniered skirt, dicky, ruff, and powdered wig,
    Beauty mole, Mohawk, or nipple ring,
The pencilled eyebrow above Fortuny pleats,
    The homeless addict's stolen parka,
Facelift, mukluk, ponytail, fez, dirndl, ascot,
    The starlet's lucite stiletto heels,
The billboard model with his briefs at half-mast,
    The geisha's obi, the gigolo's
Espadrilles, the war widow's décolletage . . .
    Any arrangement elaborates
A desire to mask that part of the world
    One's body is. Nostalgia no more
Than anarchy laces up the secondhand
    Myths we dress our well-fingered goods in.
Better still perhaps to change the body's shape
    With rings to elongate the neck, shoes
To bind the feet, lead plates wrapped to budding breasts,
    The sadhu's penis-weights and plasters,
The oiled, pumped-up torsos at Muscle Beach,

Or corsets cinched so tightly the ribs
Protrude like a smug, rutting pouter pigeon's.
    They serve to remind us we are not
Our own bodies but anagrams of their flesh,
    And pain not a feeling but a thought.

But best of all, so say fellow travellers
    In the fetish clan, is the tattoo,
Because not merely molded or worn awhile
    But exuded from the body's sense
Of itself, the story of its conjuring
    A means defiantly to round on
Death's insufferably endless emptiness.
    If cavemen smeared their bones with ochre,
The color of blood and first symbol of life,
    Then peoples ever since—Egyptian
Priestesses, Mayan chieftains, woady Druids,
    Scythian nomads and Hebrew slaves,
Praetorian guards and kabuki actors,
    Hell's Angels, pilgrims, monks, and convicts—
Have marked themselves or been forcibly branded
    To signify that they are members
Of a group apart, usually above
    But often below the rest of us.
The instruments come effortlessly to hand:
    Fish bone, razor blade, bamboo sliver,
Thorn, glass, shell shard, nail, or electric needle.
    The canvas is pierced, the lines are drawn,
The colors suffuse a pattern of desire.
    The Eskimos pull a charcoaled string
Beneath the skin, and seadogs used to cover
    The art with gunpowder and set fire
To it. The explosion drove the colors in.

Teddy boys might use matchtip sulfur
Or caked shoe polish mashed with spit. In Thailand
    The indigo was once a gecko.
In mall parlors here, India ink and tabs
    Of pigment cut with grain alcohol
Patch together tribal grids, vows, fantasies,
    Frescoes, planetary signs, pinups,
Rock idols, bar codes, all the insignia
    Of the brave face and the lonely heart.

The reasons are both remote and parallel.
    The primitive impulse was to join,
The modern to detach oneself from, the world.
    The hunter's shadowy camouflage,
The pubescent girl's fertility token,
    The warrior's lurid coat of mail,
The believer's entrée to the afterlife—
    The spiritual practicality
Of our ancestors remains a source of pride.
    Yielding to sentimentality,
Later initiates seek to dramatize
    Their jingoism, their Juliets
Or Romeos. They want to fix a moment,
    Some port of call, a hot one-night-stand,
A rush of mother-love or Satan worship.
    Superstition prompts the open eye
On the sailor's lid, the fish on his ankle.
    The biker makes a leather jacket
Of his soft beer belly and nail-bitten hands.
    The call girl's strategic butterfly
Or calla lily attracts and focuses
    Her client's interest and credit card.

But whether encoded or flaunted, there's death
  At the bottom of every tattoo.
The mark of Cain, the stigma to protect him
  From the enemy he'd created,
Must have been a skull. Once incorporated,
  Its spell is broken, its mortal grip
Loosened or laughed at or fearlessly faced down.
  A Donald Duck with drooping forelock
And swastikas for eyes, the sci-fi dragon,
  The amazon's ogress, the mazy
Yin-yang dragnets, the spiders on barbed-wire webs,
  The talismanic fangs and jesters,
Ankhs and salamanders, scorpions and dice,
  All are meant to soothe the savage breast
Or back beneath whose dyed flesh there beats something
  That will stop. Better never to be
Naked again than not disguise what time will
  Press like a flower in its notebook,
Will score and splotch, rot, erode, and finish off.
  Ugly heads are raised against our end.
If others are unnerved, why not death itself?
  If unique, then why not immortal?
Protected by totem animals that perch
  Or coil in strategic locations—
A lizard just behind the ear, a tiger's
  Fangs seeming to rip open the chest,
An eagle spreading its wings across the back—
  The body at once both draws death down
And threatens its dominion. The pain endured
  To thwart the greater pain is nothing
Next to the notion of nothingness.
  Is that what I see in the mirror?
The vacancy of everything behind me,

The eye that now takes so little in,
The unmarked skin, the soul without privileges . . .
    Everything's exposed to no purpose.
The tears leave no trace of their grief on my face.
    My gifts are never packaged, never
Teasingly postponed by the need to undo
    The puzzled perfections of surface.
All over I am open to whatever
    You may make of me, and death soon will,
Its unmarked grave the shape of things to come,
    The page there was no time to write on.

3.

NEW ZEALAND, 1890

Because he was the chieftain's eldest son
            And so himself
        Destined one day to rule,
The great meetinghouse was garishly strung
        With smoked heads and armfuls
Of flax, the kiwi cloak, the lithograph
Of Queen Victoria, seated and stiff,

Oil lamps, the greenstone clubs and treasure box
            Carved with demons
        In polished attitudes
That held the tribal feathers and ear drops.
        Kettles of fern root, stewed

Dog, mulberry, crayfish and yam were hung
To wait over the fire's spluttering tongues.

The boy was led in. It was the last day
          Of his ordeal.
      The tenderest sections—
Under his eyes, inside his ears—remained
      To be cut, the maze run
To its dizzying ends, a waterwheel
Lapping his flesh the better to reveal

Its false-face of unchanging hostility.
          A feeding tube
      Was put between his lips.
His arms and legs were held down forcibly.
      Resin and lichen, mixed
With pigeon fat and burnt to soot, was scooped
Into mussel shells. The women withdrew.

By then the boy had slowly turned his head,
          Whether to watch
      Them leave or keep his eye
On the stooped, grayhaired cutter who was led
      In amidst the men's cries
Of ceremonial anger at each
Of the night's cloudless hours on its path

Through the boy's life. The cutter knelt beside
      The boy and stroked

The new scars, the smooth skin.
From his set of whalebone chisels he tied
         The shortest one with thin
Leather thongs to a wooden handle soaked
In rancid oil. Only his trembling throat

Betrayed the boy. The cutter smiled and took
              A small mallet,
         Laid the chisel along
The cheekbone, and tapped so a sharpness struck
         The skin like a bygone
Memory of other pain, other threats.
Someone dabbed at the blood. Someone else led

A growling chant about their ancestors.
              Beside the eye's
         Spongy marshland a frond
Sprouted, a jagged gash to which occurs
         A symmetrical form,
While another chisel pecks in the dye,
A blue the deep furrow intensifies.

The boy's eyes are fluttering now, rolling
              Back in his head.
         The cutter stops only
To loop the blade into a spiralling,
         Astringent filigree
Whose swollen tracery, it seems, has led
The boy beyond the living and the dead.

He can feel the nine Nothings drift past him
         In the dark: Night,
     The Great Night, the Choking
Night, the All-Brightening Night and the Dim,
     The Long Night, the Floating
Night, the Empty Night, and with the first light
A surging called the War Canoe of Night—

Which carries Sky Father and Earth Mother,
         Their six sons borne
     Inside the airless black
The two make, clasped only to each other.
     Turning onto his back,
The eldest son struggles with all his force,
Shoulder to sky, straining until it's torn

Violently away from the bleeding earth.
         He sets four beams,
     Named for the winds, to keep
His parents apart. They're weeping, the curve
     Of loneliness complete
Between them now. The old father's tears gleam
Like stars, then fall as aimlessly as dreams

To earth, which waits for them all to return.
         Hers is the care
     Of the dead, and his tears
Seep into her folds like a dye that burns.
     One last huge drop appears
Hanging over the boy's head. Wincing, scared,
He's put his hand up into the cold air.

II.

PIBROCH

But now that I am used to pain,
Its knuckles in my mouth the same
Today as yesterday, the cause
As clear-obscure as who's to blame,

A fascination with the flaws
Sets in—the plundered heart, the pause
Between those earnest, oversold
Liberties that took like laws.

What should have been I never told,
Afraid of outbursts you'd withhold.
Why are desires something to share?
I'm shivering, though it isn't cold.

Beneath your window, I stand and stare.
The planets turn. The trees are bare.
I'll toss a pebble at the pane,
But softly, knowing you are not there.

A D E N

Rimbaud dying

His room. His room is a burning aquarium.
The moon has set. The click of prayer beads
Soothes someone's panic downstairs.
Any minute now the sun's evil eye
Will peer through the packing-crate shutters
To settle on a scale hung from the ceiling.

The indifferent day stretches out on rawhide
And chews its qat. The bandage is sweating,
His leg is sweating, his knee now swollen
To the size of a skull. Angels in his veins
Weep for their empty sabbath and loot his sorrows.
Stalls in the Market of Silence open next door.

The world is happening again without him.
Grit's blown up onto the trussed sharks.
Two subalterns in topees are arguing.
Dhows at the wharf, gharries at the curb,
Mongrels and hawkers and slops in the shade.
The black boy beside him whispers *"Mektoub."*

Where is forgiveness? A hand is stroking
His head, the fingers like albino carp

Gliding aimlessly through his hair,
Brushing sometimes against the fever-weed.
Where is forgiveness? Sleep with your eyes open,
Sleep on the stone you have made of your heart.

Here at the end—Death clumsy as an old priest—
Some words, some oil, a thin broth of memory . . .
Lying at night in a waving wheatfield, face to face
With the sky's black icon. The stars are moving too.
They rustle like a silk in whose pleats are kept
The changes: flesh to flame, ash to air.

MOTETS

THE AGAVE

The villa's switchback garden path,
between the potted railing and the sea
and under the canopy of overlapping pines,
winds through what can grow under them:
plants from a moon orbiting Venus maybe,
brambly fig, yucca, holm oak, firethorn,
and silvery, bloated succulents—
The Penitent, Dead-Child's-Fingers,
Mother's-Stool, Chapel-of-Solitude.

The agave beside the stone bench,
where I have sat heavily all day,
reaches out in all directions,
its meaty, grizzled leaves each
the length of a man, each edged
with back-turned venomous thorns,
thumbnail billhooks in ranks down
from the empurpled spike at its tip.
The largest leaf, right next to me,
has so bent under itself, the spike
has come around and gone up through
another part of itself—the heart, say,
or whatever comes to as much as that.

Yesterday the gardener told me
it could take thirty years for the spike
slowly—never meaning to, thinking
it was headed towards the water-glare
it mistook for the little light that kept
not coming from above—slowly
to pierce its own flesh, to sink its sorrow
deep within and through its own life.

It only took me a month.

THE FEVER

The fever has lasted three days.
Layers of skins and weavings
were first heaped on the bed
but nothing kept out the cold
that shook my body
like a crackhead mother
angry because her baby
won't stop crying.
Then another body crawled in
beside me, held me—
she throws the blue baby
down the furnace chute,
the ceiling hisses at
the ice pack's beaded apathy,
the hidden air, the voices,
the voices all too calm.
I'm hauled up, they listen
to my back. What can it say?
They listen to my front.
A deep breath. Does this hurt?
So much I can't answer.
They ease me back down.
The one beside me slips away.
I can hear him in the next room.
He's laughing. He's given up.

This is how love feels, they write.
So which one am I in love with?

THE INFECTION

In those days I used to refuse the medicine
because the infection then made it hurt so
when I came, hurt so that the pain—
its intolerable scalding contractions,
the knot choked by appetite, desperate
to advance and retreat, to thrash further
inside its own swollen sentence,
the little useless gash, the bitter spasm—
each night left me frightened and smiling.
The tears had rinsed my eyes, the whining
stilled any desire to repeat myself.
I thought of it as a kind of mutilation,
less of my body than of my longing not to have one.
Afterwards, I would limp to the bathroom
for a hot washcloth and hold it to myself,
and then to my face. The cloth smelled
of the rotten hyacinths, their stalks snapped,
their milky petals gone brown and sticky,
I would pass each weekend, thrown to the back
of the stalls, pots of them, at the flower market.
I went to the window, put the cloth on the stone
ledge. Until it dried, it would be my standard,
my scorn and seamark, my flag of surrender.

THE CEMETERY

After a month, it seemed like forever.
I'd find myself in the afternoons
at the municipal cemetery,
near one of the league-long colonnades
of sealed drawers and plastic flowers.
Was it a monument or a warning?
A life-size woman in limestone,
listening at the grate of an iron door,
her face half-turned towards the figure
at her feet—a beggar? the little love-boy
in rags, dirty with the years gone by?
In one hand she holds a goblet
the snake twisting around her arm drinks from.
In the other, a shallow bowl filled with coins.
She is spilling the coins towards the boy,
his arm reaching up, fingers pleading.
The stone coins have spilled over the bowl,
falling towards the boy who never gets them.

LATE AFTERNOON, ROME

Down the street, on the path to the oratory,
the stations of the cross—huge bronze slabs,
their ordinary agonies modernized to poses
on a fashion runway—have been wired shut.
A river of swallows sheers off course again
around air-locked spurs of warmth or chill.
The sun is out late, panning for gold
in the silt of our ochre upper floors.
Everything is looking up for a change.
Isn't that white capsule on the blue tablecloth
the daily jumbo jet? It's so far beyond
the cross and thorns, beyond the drawstring
of birds, beyond the last light down here.
And there's already a glass of water on the table,
for the pill I was meant to take hours ago.

THE BOOKCASE

My empty bookcase yawns and rises
from its paint job, white asphalt
newly laid over a grid of back streets,
the chill of what assurance supports it all
still in the air, no music, no voices.
Who wants to live with what he knows?
While I sit on the storage boxes,
my double's slowly making his way
among shop windows and bloody altars,
holding pages to the light, changing
sex to distance himself from force
or faithfulness, the household demons.
It's late. Opportunities are multiplying.
I am what I did? I am what I wait for?
I feel something returning, like a book
put back on the shelf, slid between
names like mine, my story, my fault.

YEAR'S END

This afternoon—an uprush of late November
mildness—I cut down the garden stragglers,
the knotty rose hips and bone-dry pods,
the jaundiced hosta, the lavender, a few
still unblasted, stupidly hopeful annuals.
In the beds, new moon-bleeding branches
had fallen, and leaves blown through slats
in the sky, morning wind, evening wind.
It's time for Caesar's head to be wrapped
in its black plastic bag and duct tape,
and thrown into winter's trunk.
I hate the distant words that brought this on:
seed   orbit   pattern   increase   triumph.
But at least the choking has stopped,
the siege been raised, the old heads bent
by the fireplace now, explaining
the mob's breath, the rider's dew,
one shadow fallen onto another,
the streaming golden hair on the corpse
dragged again around the city walls,
and snow about to cover them all.

THE NEWS

By seven the old women were leaving
the cathedral's side door, behind them
Christ in a fringed paisley loincloth
and the flaring spray of gold and silver
votive hearts, hundreds of them,
like drops of blood shaken from his face,
and a handful of men were clustered
around the zocalo's only newsstand
to read about the government scandal
on the front page of the morning paper
hung up on a wire with clothespins,
beneath which, on the vendor's plastic table,
are stacked the rows of pornographic
comic books whose covers work
their variations on last night's fantasies:
the two muscled thugs who lick the thighs
of a moaning, blindfolded schoolgirl,
and a winking amazon in lace armor
who kicks her pursuer, pants around his knees,
in the balls. Up and down. In and out.
That old scandal. The flesh corrupted
with pleasure and punished with more.

RAIN ROOM

For days it had been wet and wetter.
The swanned moat, the drowned cypresses,
the great lawn's obligations to water—
everything finally ready for it to sink in.
Our hosts asked that we amuse ourselves
in the rain room, with its lacquered
snippets and chests of game boards.
We decided to try an old favorite
and took out the pain-by-numbers.
The pug was curled in a window seat.
A local train pouted in the distance.
You did the blues, I did the reds.
You did the hectic lake, a stand of pines,
the cold shoulder and dull threats.
I did the chimney and dead elms,
the frayed, silken cords of scorn.
I did the night away from home
and each of the three conditions.
The reconciliation we left blank
and put away the faithful brushes.
Look at the picture of us now,
the little landscape of a life together.
Who'd have guessed what we forgot?
The willow has no reflection, the barn
no door. And in an upper-storey window
of the house, you can just make out
a shadowy figure in the glass's flutter,
someone looking out at the rain,
alone inside an idea gone wrong.

THE MODEL

The model lay on a sheet
trimmed with silver lacery,
a lopsided strand of pearls
around her neck, her eyes
half open to everything, her hair
pulled behind, one loose tangle
fallen over her left shoulder.
Her torso had been peeled back
from breast to patch, lifted off.
There she was, at last herself.
Her heart still glistened
with its suppliant runners,
its black veins getting nowhere.
The sheath of liver, the back streets
of gutwork, those crimped
or lustrously blistered globes
they were trying to stuff back in.
And the tucked fetus, as clean
and small as a wince, a wire.
Where will they put that?
To whom does it belong now?

HOTEL BAR

The saxophonist winds up "My Romance,"
the song with a scar. In the red lacquer ceiling,
the night's raw throat, I can just make out
lampshades the color of a smoker's breath.
One is at our table. Across sits a woman
in tiny furs from before the war, the mouth
of one gnawing on the tail of the other,
like comets. A sudden brightness on stage,
a flaring spot, flashes on the nodding brass.
The little thud at a nova's heart predicts
the gradual, dimming ebb and flow
of light—or love—soon enough burnt out,
remembered only as desire's afterglow.
So which one has the room key? Neither of us
wants to guess what won't ever be opened.
Something is found in a galactic pocket.
Something is left behind on a chair.
The elevator doors close soundlessly.
A constellation of numbers rises in order.
Again, the argument from design's invoked.
Tomorrow we'll get to go back over it all,
what's partially false and almost always true,
as in "My romance doesn't need a thing but you."

LEXINGTON AVENUE
SUBWAY, 1941

And on the way to somewhere else—
he can't think of the stop, the stops
are quiet, strangers turning in the light—
he's leaned back against the window,
against the glazed leaves, the chips
of seablue and skygold, the platform's
map of boundaries the rain changes
while through the grate the upper world,
on its own iron wheels, is sidetracked
towards history's fenced-in yard, and shut
his eyes to imagine that, years from now,
he is sitting beside himself, the dream's
train of thought pulling the figure forward
from all the disappointments. There he is.
He'll ask this nerveless dark angel of age
again what he did, what he did wrong.

How could you know what your father
would never admit, what your mother
would never accept? How could you know
their own fears were your child-bed,
your small, high window onto the city?
The unwelcome advice, the useless clarity,
the small passions, how confusing
all the ideas of others turned out to be.
The woman you married, the other men
she came to love more, the only son
you haven't seen because he wanted any life
but the one you gave him to throw away. . . .

The parts have been worked out for us,
and you pause as if by accident
and try to recall just what it was
she said in the doorway. Was she angry?

A TOUR OF THE VOLCANO

After colliding with a cloudberg, the chopper
sinks through more, like feelings gone soft
around the edges, forming shapeless moist
masses and as easily dissolving, until underhead
we approach the ashen, lopsided cones,
the brimstone stench of steam, the mess of gods.
Headphones dip into the sliding plates
dragged over soft forces divided by stress,
some fracturing crust of indifference
through which the buried magma seeps.
Or have I got it all wrong again?
Does he mean instead that, once home,
after we're back, set down, driven off,
the sunset's backwash sloshing
in the rearview's little sac of sorrows,
the tremors will start again, the leakage?

HAPPINESS

As ghosts are said to do, hadn't we searched
helplessly for places we imagined having been
happy in? You went north, I went south
through the daybook's scrawl, the zest
flossed from two back teeth, a clock as round
as the earth hanging from a bronze fish,
a swell of Brahms, a shirt on the floor,
the poppers and handcuffs, the circularities
of the sun and moon through stages
of boredom or rapture, the very idea
of the two of us, together for so long
without knowing we were supposed to be.

Seen from the angle of solitude now,
how we trembled at empty terrors, or made
ourselves miserable with false fancies.
But the happiness—it hardened the heart
because we thought we deserved its idleness.
Now all we have are shapes on the sheet,
yours doubled over, mine clenched and released.

IN THE VALLEY

The day's long since broken and light's
spilled over the lip of heat in the valley.
Small desires come to mind and go,
their going at least a cold taste
of what's on the horizon this next leg
along the trail our affair has blazed.
These markers—the stack of stones
from whose thirst-crazed throat?
the blue arrow hastily painted
on rock with whose knotted anger?—
have led me along a story line.
The cactus, the scrub, the serrated
glare have their own bit parts in it.
Like me, the dead river thrives
on an old lack of purpose and follows
a useless way, snaking around
obstacles too long gone even to be
missed. The violence of the place
seems fragile, as if overly logical.
Everything repeats itself. Behind
this cloud, beside that boulder
is another and another. Each step
away from them echoes the original
inertia, or the first time I winced—
at what? the kiss? the strap? the stitch?
The old room smears. Left to myself,
hour by hour, the heat erases everything
but a sense of its unbearable persuasions.

Okay, I'll walk until the sun goes down
numbly on the world and the sky's
chokehold forces me to consider
the sweat beads on the night's torso,
the edge of the new moon's cock ring,
even last year's losing streak crossing
through the black etceteras.
It's so hard to tell the time. The dial
keeps staring back at me unmoved,
just the tsk-tsk of its second hand
and its phosphorescent treadmill.
Hadn't I set out to learn what hurts and why?
You know the reason when you pull back
from a scalding thrill or sumptuary weight.
You know love in the definitions: What feels
its way blindly over the strange body.
What turns its face too soon, too late.

FOUR DAYS

The four days after your call have been steel
engravings, their acids eating into black
particles of the past and waves of future
shock. First, the sheaves harvested
to be beaten by boys with wings, watched
by a hidden camera's own bored abundance
steady on your shield and key.
The next day, I'm pinned to my rock,
its canopy of squalls, the torn gut,
while in the higher clouds your sleds
are drawn by little engines of ego,
mechanical peacocks laying blame,
all strut and screech and widened eye.
By the third day the forge is lit
and the old muscled gods, their armor
put aside, are playing with fire.
They're busy hammering arrowheads
for whoever is meant to aim at me,
an old look-alike or new musketeer.
And last of all, today, sobering up
in the shower, the echoes crackling
my shell, I'm halfway up a rope ladder.
I hear slapping bilge and luffing sail.
I can reach on deck for the rudder.
Everything steadies. It feels like a phone.

Visiting the Dead

The way down was difficult enough
without wondering what I would find,
the river of years having grown wider,
the jars of blood threatening to spill over,
rows of the long unburied spitting curses,
the purebred to be slaughtered and salted
twice bolting, the fragile stick figures
in my pack jammed in with the mirrors
and strigils, the herbs and honey cups—
whatever gift might become the gift of speech.

Near the end, I shaved my head and wore
a necktie, hoping he would recognize me.
Gradually, from behind a shooting fall
of soot, my father appeared, a decade gone.
He edged closer, expressionless,
gaunt, pomaded, a thin mustache
he'd acquired since, and on his chest
the lump where his pacemaker still ticked.
The featherweight of loss we bear
isn't often now in my dreams—where I want

once more to warn him a rock is giving way,
or drag him choking from the neighbor's pool—
but here he is. Photographs of him as a boy—
I have one in my kit—are myself to the life,
as he might as well be standing here, given
a few more years, a few more bad decisions.

Could I tell him I loved him? Could I ever?
He was the reason I was there, the reason
I had first entered and finally left the world.
I reached to embrace him and closed my arms on air.

LAMIA

Whatever we put in the child's crib,
the stingray tail or amber beads,
we can never be sure it will be enough.

The nurse may fall asleep and the Undercutter
slip in—the playpen, the bath, the van—
rubbing her filthy testicles and breasts

against the alarm, against the baby's face.
Everything hidden and nameless in the soul
rises to tear from us what we have made

of ourselves. She will eat what she desires.
Perhaps if we rub our spit on its forehead. . . .
But the night watches her indifferently,

watches her at the lake put the car in reverse,
watches as she draws a knife across its breath.
Her own children died, so that others must.

There it is now, dressed in white and laid out
on the marriage bed. The telephone is ringing.
There is always a reason the child is dead.

MOON PROBE

The wrinkled hand
held up—against what?
A shriveled apple
on the table—left by whom?

That far cold sphere
lodged in my chest,
how its inner core
has grown smaller
than its covering,
loosened like memories.

The stopped watch
on the bureau top
amidst a galaxy
of coins and cufflinks.
The silver's initialed:
There is no cure.

The devil's leavings
are virtue's sacrifice.
Satellites elsewhere beam
a sideways spectrum
of false colors and scale.
But you and your bowl
of black and white,
a fumarole

venting the chamber,
you are the sad truth,
which is why
we lie on our backs
in the dark and wish.

The rills of lace
around the infant's
sectioned head,
the burst seed-case
of floating
cranial nerve-ends,
the glass eyes,
the lips puckering
in the tsar's beaker
of balsamic liquor,
speechlessly teaching
the temple elders.
Even death itself
is afraid.

TWO MEN

Any two men looking love in the eye
keep a short distance between themselves—
vanes of spoked tissue furtively unfurling—
the shades drawn and overcoats on indoors,
as if under their shapelessness were all
that might somehow be wanted later on—
a lifetime's change of clothes or mind.

Still the fleshmate's solitary focus blurs
what intrusive appeal your outsider's
Look here suggests, a glancing blow
smiled at, as if on that staircase one flirt
opens, the shutter's puckered reckoning.
Any lens is an hourglass the years slip
slowly, swiftly down. May ours together

fill a future that will have come out right,
each of us, both of us, brought at last to light.

O U I J A

in memory of James Merrill

Years ago—long enough at least for bitter
Leaves to have cooled at the bottom of a cup
Then brimful and steaming with insecurities—
Four spellbound friends were huddled around
What might as well have been a campfire,
Their shadows thrown back on the world
By candlelight, the flames of anticipation
Fed by skittish questions of whatever voice
Any one of them had felt clearing its throat
Inside the jelly lid with its toothpick pointer
Patrolling a border of hand-drawn letters—

Not theirs, of course, the timidly curious
Weekend houseguests in rainy Stonington,
But JM's, the loom from which bolts of blues
Lay stacked on his desk, *Ephraim*'s final galleys.
The master had been unexpectedly
Summoned by redundancy—a family crisis—
But insisted . . . look, the steak's been marinating,
There's plenty to drink, the weather forecast's glum.
They'd stay? And why not take an idle turn
At the board? His Honda was barely in reverse
When Mickey's mop and pail were blithely tossed

Aside and motley, ill-fitting robes assumed—
In their case, a cheap imitation mantle
That, like any religion, risked mocking
What it worshiped. But then, how else learn
What can't be taught than play the earnest fool?
Left alone with a luster and delirium
About to be cut with callow, flavorless slush,
They pulled their chairs up to the round table,
Guarded by votive griffins, a saltcellar,
And a spineless cactus that waited patiently
Under a bite-size crystal hanging from the dome.

Roach clip. Jug wine. The conventional aids
To inspiration were reluctantly foresworn
In favor of seltzer and cold credulity.
They sat there edgily, hour after hour,
Watching the voices muster into words—
As when, between the scenes of a play, the stage
Is briefly darkened but still slightly visible,
Enough for us to see the stagehands moving
Furniture around, the props of what's to come—
So that what had clumsily been transcribed
Into a notebook later came clear in ways

Each might have made light of there in the dark.
A—, for instance, at thirty buffed and tan
But oddly pious and almost too eager for word
Of how immanent the Beyond would turn out to be,
A lens in the black box of lives led here below.
He begins by chance with Agul, a priest of Aton,
Standoffish and abstract. *Egyptians not concerned
With sin, only singularity. We wait for sunrise.*

Friends exchange light. Love, light, are one.
I breathe your light. Aton knows your aspect.
And for those who don't care, whose beliefs start

When their eyes are shut? *Night is sun for others.*
Doggedly the acolyte buttonholes the board.
At last one Mary Wentworth gently picks up
The extension, a London mother and mystic
Two centuries dead. *Your soul, sweet A—,*
The shape of a healthy body, shelters under my wing.
Wing? *Down is warmer than up.* Up?
The Pharisees are cold on their mountain tops.
They will not sin & so they freeze. Your body
Sins to warm your heart. How easily tenderness
Rinses the dirty hands temptation lathers.

Then B—, saddled with a Fifties adolescence
Spent peeping at encyclopedia cross-sections
And nudist colony glossies—all shrivel and sag—
Until transfixed by martyred Oscar's wit,
Its gay science devoted to curing the heart,
Shyly asks, after combing his hair, for Himself.
The Other Life, within us or abroad,
Acts—and why not?—as if it had all the time
In either world, exaggerating its courtesies.
Wilde extends an invisible gloved hand
To B—, who stutters about his nervousness.

Confession is good for one's soul & one's royalties.
I sold my lower depths & made a good thing of them.
But his own feelings . . . for the young man, say?

Bosie was ornamental. That was enough.
No real love then? Your wife? *Constance*
Was as her name suggests. That was not enough.
Though Paris is, of course, better on the whole,
I think most of Oxford, where, donning robes,
Pater drew on airy nothing to burn with a flame
Of the first water, in whose heat our damp clay
Was fired into well-wrought urnings. ("The ease,"

B— marvels, "with which a practiced stagecraft
Flicks its iridescent fan!") *No window*
Can without some dressing up long hold
A discerning eye. For birds of our feather
The pen that is a plume adds panache.
But—oh, this is as it must be written—
A thousand admiring eyes in the world
Of letters finally matter less than the one
Understanding heart in a country retreat.
Blushing, B— withdraws, interested only
In how prudently to spend his overdraft.

Then C—, whose reedy, wire-rimmed pretense,
Goosed by Southern manners and a French degree,
The saccharine-coated pill B— had been swallowing
For a decade, insinuates his clubman's smarm
And succeeds in raising static on the line.
A giggling Indian scout—*ice filled my seeing,*
Great ice-haired mounts, English—trails off
To a corpuscle who or which insists eternity
Is *the plucked tension between limit and nothing.*
A yawn gets passed around. A Chinese sage
Wanders across the screen, dropping fragments

Of a fortune cookie. *We do not gain the moon*
By telling her to be still. Fingers in silhouette
Mug redwood trees, or German armaments
Tycoon, or chef, or silent movie vamp,
The manic Cuisinart finally shredding
Soul into a slaw of nonsense syllables.
The others glower at C— and call a break,
When suddenly, as from another room,
A stricken whisper: *Was I that humpback*
At whom you laughed when you believed me
Out of hearing? Oh sweet betrayal, my bridegroom!

And D—. (But why "D—"? His name was Drew.
I knew him, loved him.) A tenant of his body,
He was hurt by everything he took for remedy—
Waiting tables, acupuncture, coke—
And longed to leap against the painted drop,
Some grand pirouette center stage, sweat whipped
Into the spotlight, sequined corsair or satyr.
He asks for Isadora. *Hail, friend!*
Why do they never book me anymore?
Drew then nudges into the dressing room
With a question. Will I ever dance like you?

You know in your bones. I died broken on the wheel
Of circumstance. Now it's just tableau vivant.
The happiness of the body is all on earth.
The beauty of the body in motion and repose
I wanted to give, long after it was probable.
Drew's charged resolve saw him through the drill
(Temp job to tryout) of making a name for himself,
Until he met the dancer who infected him.

The virus flic-flacked through his system, aswirl
In cells that faltered and too soon abandoned
The soloist whose stumble a falling curtain concealed.

For that matter, you too, JM, have gone
And done it, become a voice, letters on a page—
Not like love's sweet thoughtless routine
But a new romance, hazard and implication,
Promises as yet unmade, possibilities
Slipping, say, from N to O . . . —Oh,
Why will words cohere and dissolve on this blank
And not their darker meanings, an unspoken grief
I've reached for and felt sliding as if over
Poster board smoothed by years of being used
To giving back the bright presence drawn

Up from within yourself, your starry heart
So empty, so large, too filled with others
Not to fear an unworthiness indwelling.
You took everything on faith but death,
An old friend's or the breathless lining
Of any new encounter, so that fresh acolytes,
Once back home, would remark with wonder
On your otherworldliness. What they failed
To see was something that has just now begun
To sink in on me: how little your detachment
Had to do with the demands of a formal art

Or a mind at once too sovereign and too spent
By being trolled for schools of thought or feeling.
Stage fright can apply or smear what make-up

Seems necessary for any evening's encores,
And lines rehearsed before the smoked mirror's
Critical gaze can turn to ashes in the mouth
When spoken to some poor stick mugging there
Who you hope will stay the night and fear
May last until the end. How seldom, I sense,
You gave yourself up, how often instead
Had to borrow back what had already been lent.

Even the board is under wraps in a closet upstairs.
Funny, I've not tried to do it since you died,
Even for a simple jabbing towards the consoling *Yes*
In answer to the obvious questions posed
By missing you. Or have I instead been fearing
The *No*—the not-happy *No*, the not-there *No*?
Or had you perhaps been receding all along—
Like those friends of a quarter century ago,
Faded to vanishing points like death or California,
Where everything to be lost is finally regained,
The figures of speech for once beyond compare?

No. I *can* hear your voice from the other side,
That kingdom-come memory makes of the past,
The old recordings, the stiffening onionskin
Letters your Olivetti punched out from Athens
Or Isfahan, notebook cities shaped
By anecdotes of love—no, antidotes,
Spelled out to be kept suspended at a distance,
As now I imagine your nights with pencil and cup.
From my seat, somehow above or below the table,
Your hand moving steadily back and forth
Across the board seems like a wave goodbye.

ACKNOWLEDGMENTS

Some of the poems in this book originally appeared as follows:
Columbia: "The Cemetery," "The Model"
The James White Review: "The Infection"
Kunapipi: "Aden"
Literary Imagination: "Cancer"
London Review of Books: "Hotel Bar"
New England Review: "Fado"
The New Republic: "Late Afternoon, Rome," "The Bookcase"
The New Yorker: "A Tour of the Volcano," "Orchid,"
    "Visiting the Dead"
New York Times Book Review: "Year's End"
The Paris Review: "Tattoos"
Parnassus: "Feces"
Poetry: "Ouija," "Jihad," "Pibroch"
Raritan: "Largesse"
Solo: "Two Men"
Southwest Review: "Tankas"
Stand: "Glanum"
Times Literary Supplement (UK): "Elbows"
TriQuarterly: "Penis," "In the Valley"

"Lexington Avenue Subway, 1941," after the photograph by
    Walker Evans, first appeared in *Words for Images: A
    Gallery of Poems,* edited by John Hollander and Joanna
    Weber (Yale University Art Gallery, 2001).
"Glanum" was delivered as the 1999 Phi Beta Kappa poem
    at Yale University.

A NOTE ABOUT THE AUTHOR

J. D. McClatchy is the author of four earlier books of poems, *Scenes from Another Life* (1981), *Stars Principal* (1986), *The Rest of the Way* (1990), and *Ten Commandments* (1998). His literary essays are collected in *White Paper* (1989) and *Twenty Questions* (1998). He is the editor of *The Vintage Book of Contemporary American Poetry* (1990) and *The Vintage Book of Contemporary World Poetry* (1996), as well as a co-editor of James Merrill's *Collected Poems* (2001) and *Collected Novels and Plays* (2002). The author of several opera libretti, McClatchy is a chancellor of the Academy of American Poets and a member of the American Academy of Arts and Letters. He teaches at Yale University and is editor of *The Yale Review.*

A NOTE ON THE TYPE

The text of this book was set in Century Schoolbook, one of several variations of Century Roman to appear within a decade of its creation. The original Century Roman face was cut by Linn Boyd Benton (1844–1932) in 1895, in response to a request by Theodore Low De Vinne for an attractive, easy-to-read typeface to fit the narrow columns of his *Century Magazine.*

Century Schoolbook was specifically designed for school textbooks in the primary grades, but its great legibility quickly earned it popularity in a range of applications. Century remains the only American face cut before 1910 that is still widely in use today.

Composed by Creative Graphics, Inc.,
Allentown, Pennsylvania
Printed and bound by United Book Press, Inc.,
Baltimore, Maryland
Designed by Chip Kidd